100 GAMES
OF LOGIC

Also by Pierre Berloquin

100 Perceptual Puzzles
100 Numerical Games

Pierre Berloquin

100 GAMES
OF LOGIC

Foreword by Martin Gardner
Drawings by Denis Dugas

BARNES
&NOBLE
BOOKS
NEW YORK

Contents

Foreword

Pierre Berloquin, who put together this stimulating and delightful collection of mind benders, is a clever young Frenchman who was born in 1939 in Tours and graduated in 1962 from the Ecole Nationale Supérieure des Mines in Paris. His training as an operations research engineer gave him an excellent background in mathematics and logical thinking.

But Berloquin was more interested in writing than in working on operations research problems. After two years with a Paris advertising agency, he decided to try his luck at freelance writing and this is how he has earned his living since. In 1964 he began his popular column on "Games and Paradoxes" in the magazine *Science et Vie* (Science and Life). Another column, "From a Logical Point of View," appears twice monthly in *The World of Science*, a supplement of the Paris newspaper *Le Monde*. Occasionally he contributes to other French magazines. One of his favorite avocations is leading groups of "*créativité*," a French cocktail of brainstorming, synectics, and encounter therapy, for the discovery of new ideas and the solution of problems—a logical extension of his interest in puzzles.

Berloquin's published books are *Le Livre des jeux* (card and board games), *Le Livre des divertissements* (party games), *Le jeu de Tarot* (Tarot card game), *Testez votre intelligence* (intelligence tests), *100 grandes réussites* (solitaire games), *Un souvenir d'enfance d'Evariste Galois* (Memoir of the Childhood of Evariste Galois); he is co-author of *Voulez-vous jouer avec nous* (Come Play with Us) and *100 jeux de cartes classiques* (card games).

This volume is Berloquin's own translation into English of one of his four paperback collections of brainteasers which have been enormously popular in France and Italy since they were published in Paris in 1973. This one is concerned only with logical puzzles. The other three contain numerical, geometrical, and alphabetical problems. Denis Dugas, the graphic artist who illustrated all four books, is one of the author's old friends.

The puzzles in this collection have been carefully selected or designed (many are original with the author or artist) so that they will not be too difficult for the average reader who is not a mathematician to solve, and at the same time not be *too* easy. They are all crisply, clearly given, accurately answered at the back of the book, and great fun to work on whether you crack them or not.

At present, Berloquin is living in Neuilly, a Paris suburb, with his wife, Annie, and their two children.

MARTIN GARDNER

100 GAMES
OF LOGIC

PROBLEMS

Game 1

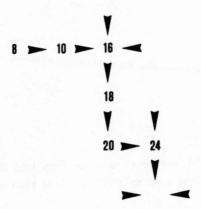

What number belongs in the empty space between the three arrows?

Game 2

Two bars of iron lie on a table. They look identical, but one of them is magnetized (with a pole at each end), and the other is not.

How can you discover which bar is magnetized if you are only allowed to shift them on the table, without raising them and without the help of any other object or instrument?

Game 3

These words follow a logical progression:

> SPHINX
> LISTEN
> TALION

Which of these could be next?

> AUREOLE
> SPROUT
> IODINE
> PROTON

Game 4

The four drawings about the duel are not in the right order. Please correct.

GAMES OF LOGIC

Game 5

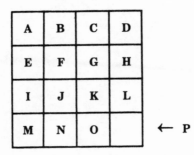

This first diagram is incomplete. Obviously, the letters are entered in alphabetical order, so the empty square gets a P.

The second diagram has been filled according to a different logical principle. Which letters go in the empty squares?

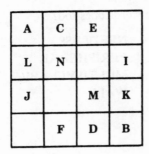

Game 6

These words belong to the same logical family:

BASSOON
ADDRESS
CORRALLED
SUCCESSIVE
FOOTHILL

Which of these words does too?

NEEDLESS
PERIPHERAL
MULTISYLLABIC
WALL

Game 7

If LEAH is LOUIS's sister,
if CLARISSE is BRUNO's sister,
if MAUD is CHRISTOPHER's sister,
then who is HAMILTON's sister—

IRENE, CLAIRE, SUE, or PEGGY?

Game 8

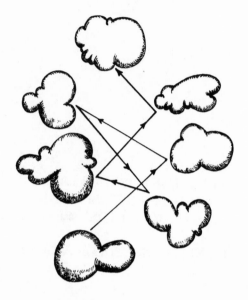

The first illustration shows how seven clouds can be placed in logical order: the first cloud has two curves; the second, three curves; and so on up to eight curves.

In the second illustration the logical principle is not too different from the first. Can you discover it? Show the logical wig sequence with arrows.

Game 9

These words follow a logical progression:

DRAMA
RABBI
CYCLE
IDLED
TENSE
AFFIX

Which of these could be next?

HATCH
FLUTE
MEDIA
WIGGLE

Game 10

The family gathering consists of father, mother, son, daughter, brother, sister, cousin, nephew, niece, uncle, and aunt. But only two men and two women are present. They have a common ancestor, and there has been no consanguine marriage.

Explain.

Game 11

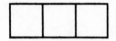

Find a common English three-letter word, knowing that:

LEG has no common letter with it.
ERG has one common letter, not at the correct place.
SIR has one common letter, at the correct place.
SIC has one common letter, not at the correct place.
AIL has one common letter, not at the correct place.

Game 12

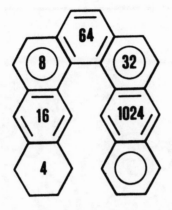

What number belongs in the empty circle?

Game 13

Five of the flowers in the vase belong to the same logical family. One is an intruder—which one, and why?

GAMES OF LOGIC

Game 14

Timothy's tie rack boasts 17 blue ties, 11 yellow, 9 orange, 34 green, and 2 violet, not sorted by color.

The light bulb has burned out. Timothy cannot see what color the ties are.

How many ties does Timothy have to take to be sure he has at least two ties of the same color?

Game 15

These words follow a logical progression:

> ABROAD
> BLONDE
> LANCER
> ACCORD
> CHORDS

Which of these could be next?

> HARASS
> HERPES
> OLDISH
> MARKER

Game 16

An accident has just occurred. The drawings are out of order—please correct.

Game 17

C A B C A B
B A B C A C
A C A B B A
C B A C C B
B A C B A C
C B A C B A

The letters are arranged according to a logical principle. What principle?

Game 18

These words belong to the same logical family:

UNDECEIVABLE
SIMULTANEOUS
ALIMENTATION
CAUTIOUSNESS
GLADIATORIAL
FORAMINIFERA

Which of these words does too?

PHILANTHROPY
SEISMOLOGIST
ONOMATOPOEIA
REAPPEARANCE

Game 19

You have been been playing "heads or tails" and you discover that your opponent is cheating. He chooses heads most of the time, for his coin has two heads.

Knowing this, you bet enough to win your money back in one more toss of his. You don't want to take the risk of demonstrating that he is a cheater. So what do you do to win?

Game 20

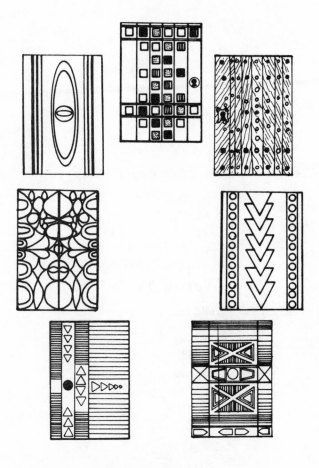

As in Game 8, there is a logical principle by which the seven doors can be put in order.

What is it? What order should they be in?

Game 21

These words follow a logical progression:

> SUNKEN
> MONASTICISM
> TUESDAY
> WEDGIES
> THUMB-SUCKER
> FRIVOLITY

Which of these could be next?

> SQUANDER
> SATIATE
> MINE
> TABLE

Game 22

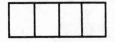

Find a common English four-letter word, knowing that each of these four words have two letters in common with it, which are not at the correct places:

> EGIS
> PLUG
> LOAM
> ANEW

Game 23

Six of the houses belong to the same logical family. One is an intruder—which one, and why?

Game 24

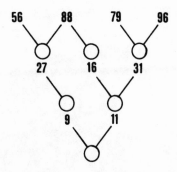

What number belongs below the bottom circle?

Game 25

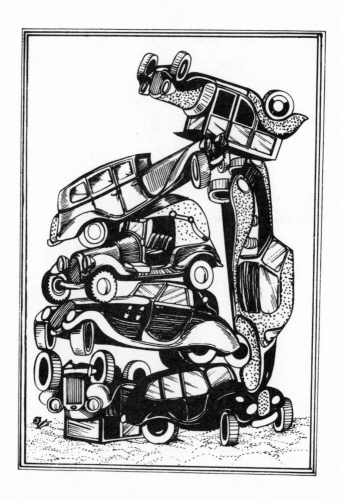

Six of the cars belong to the same logical family. One is an intruder—which one, and why?

GAMES OF LOGIC

Game 26

An inflatable boat is floating in a swimming pool. Which will raise the water level higher:

Throwing a coin into the boat?
Throwing a coin into the water?

Game 27

These words follow a logical progression:

BOXER
ELATE
RATER
OLIVE
HOTEL
ALIVE

Which of these could be next?

DUCAL
IMAGE
HASTE
MEANS

Game 28

Timothy is at the barber's. The drawings are out of order
—please correct.

Game 29

A	A	C	A	E	A
B	B	B	D	B	E
A	C	C	C	D	
D	B	D	C		
A	E	B			
F	A				

← ?

Can you complete the square logically?

Game 30

These words belong to the same logical family:

ACREAGE
LEGEND
CARPENTER
MACERATION
CARMINE
SURFACE
TENANT

Which of these words does too?

LIMITATION
ASHORE
MANNER
NEED

Game 31

Every morning Timothy, Urban, and Vincent run cross-country before breakfast.

After a month they realize that Timothy has finished before Urban more often than after him and that Urban has finished before Vincent more often than after him.

Is it possible that Vincent has finished before Timothy more often than after him?

Game 32

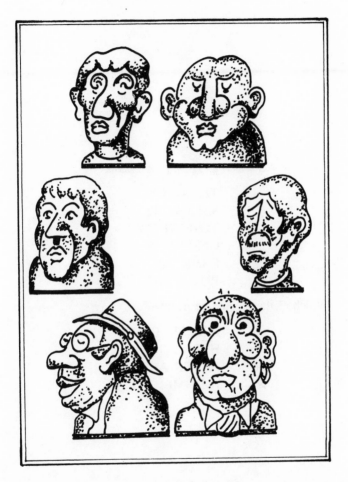

The six heads can be put in order according to a logical principle.

What is it? What order should they be in?

Game 33

These words follow a logical progression:

> TRUSTFUL
> SALTWORT
> TOMORROW
> OFFENDER
> EXERTION
> ROYALIST

Which of these could be next?

> PEDIGREE
> HYPNOTIC
> ARTERIAL
> JUDGMENT

Game 34

Find a common English five-letter word, knowing that:

ADULT has two letters in common with it, not at their correct places.

GUSTO has no common letter with it.

STORY has one common letter, at the correct place.

BUILT has one common letter, at the correct place.

DYING has one common letter, not at the correct place.

BUGLE has two common letters, but only one at the correct place.

LIGHT has no common letter with it.

Game 35

Five friends, Andrew, Bernard, Claude, Donald, and Eugene, each have a son and a daughter. Their families are so close that each has married his daughter to the son of one of his friends, and as a result the daughter-in-law of the father of Andrew's son-in-law is the sister-in-law of Bernard's son, and the son-in-law of the father of Claude's daughter-in-law is the brother-in-law of Donald's daughter.

But although the daughter-in-law of the father of Bernard's daughter-in-law has the same mother-in-law as the son-in-law of the father of Donald's son-in-law, the situation is simplified by the fact that no daughter-in-law is the sister-in-law of the daughter of her father-in-law.

Who married Eugene's daughter?

Game 36

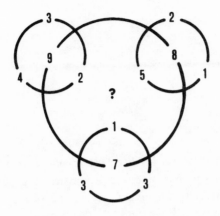

What number belongs in the center?

Game 37

Timothy notes that his five best friends do not know one another. To get things started he invites three of them to lunch: Adams, Brown, and Carter. (The two other friends are Dickinson and Emerson.) The five first names are, in no particular order, Alex, Bob, Chip, Dave, and Elmer.

After the lunch Timothy lists the results:
- Bob still does not know Brown.
- Chip knows Adams.
- Dave knows only one of the others.
- Elmer knows three of the others.
- Alex knows two of the others.
- Dickinson knows only one of the others.
- Emerson knows three of the others.

What is the full name of each of the five?

Game 38

A man sits on a buoy floating in a swimming pool. In his right hand is a glass containing an ice cube. If he throws the ice cube into the swimming pool, when will the water level rise?

- When the cube falls into the water?
- Or not until the cube is completely melted?

Game 39

These words follow a logical progression:

> TOOTHSOME
> FORECAST
> SIXTINE
> ATONAL

Which of these could be next?

> SUMMER
> BOAT
> TENDERNESS
> TYPICAL

Game 40

Andrew, Bernard, Claude, Donald, and Eugene have summer houses along the Atlantic coast.

Each wanted to name his house after the daughter of one of his friends—that is, Anne, Belle, Cecilia, Donna, and Eve (but not necessarily in that order).

To be sure that their houses would have different names the friends met to make their choices together.

Claude and Bernard both wanted to name their house Donna. They drew lots and Bernard won. Claude named his house Anne.

Andrew named his house Belle.

Eve's father hadn't come, and Eugene phoned to tell him to name his house Cecilia.

Belle's father named his house Eve.

What is the name of each friend's daughter? What is the name of his house?

Game 41

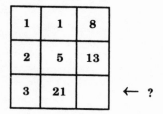

1	1	8
2	5	13
3	21	

← ?

Can you complete the square logically?

Game 42

These words belong to the same logical family:

> AFGHAN
> INDEFINITELY
> SYNOPSIS
> STUPENDOUS
> BURST

Which of these words does too?

> GLACIAL
> COMPANION
> RESCRIPT
> HIJACKER

Game 43

At an international conference there are twenty-one who speak French, twenty-one who speak English, and twenty-one who speak German. But there are much fewer than sixty-three conferees, since some of them speak several languages. In fact, all the possibilities are represented: some speak one language, some speak two, and some speak all three.

If those who speak a specific language are called a group, then, within that group, those who speak a specific two languages (like those who speak only that language, and those who speak all three languages) are called a subgroup.

Each subgroup of a given group contains a different number of persons (at least three). The largest subgroup is made up of those who speak only French.

How many speak English and German but not French?

Game 44

The seven vases can be put in order according to a logical principle.

What is it? What order should they be in?

Game 45

These words follow a logical progression:

> AUSTRALIA
> RAISIN
> CREASE
> PATOIS
> VIRTUOSO

Which of these could be next?

> MAIN
> SCHISM
> GRANITOID
> GENEROUS

Game 46

- No strategist, if he is a good tactician, can lose a battle.
- An audacious strategist does not fail to have the confidence of his troops.
- No bad tactician has the confidence of his troops.
- Women despise only the vanquished.

If the preceding statements are taken as true, can an audacious strategist be despised by women?

Game 47

Six men, A, B, C, D, E, and F, for short, and their mothers live in a village.

Each mother was widowed and has married as her second husband one of the men other than her son.

Mrs. D points out to C's mother that, by marriage, she (Mrs. D) has become the great-grandmother of Mrs. E, A has become B's stepgrandfather, and Mrs. F is the daughter-in-law of Mrs. C's granddaughter-in-law.

Who married whom?

Game 48

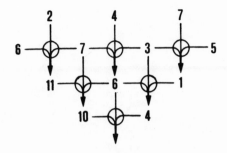

What number belongs under the bottom arrow?

Game 49

Five friends with suitable names—Doe, Deer, Hare, Boar, and Roe—are coming back from a hunting party with five animals of the same names; each has killed one animal, *not* corresponding to his own name, and each has missed another differently named animal, again not corresponding to his own name.

- The deer was killed by the hunter who has the name of the animal killed by Roe.
- The doe was killed by the hunter who has the name of the animal missed by Hare.
- Deer, who missed a roe, was very disappointed to kill only a hare.

Who killed what?

Game 50

An Oriental prince, a great lover of chess, is on his deathbed and worries about the fate of his immense fortune. To which of his three sons should it go?

His fortune is in the form of a chess set made of diamonds and rubies.

He decides that his fortune will go to the son who plays exactly half as many games of chess as the prince has days left to live.

The oldest son refuses, saying he does not know how long his father will live.

The second son refuses for the same reason.

The youngest son accepts. How does he respect his father's desires?

Game 51

These words follow a logical progression:

      PHILOSOPHICOSOCIOLOGICALLY
      ZOO
      CHRONOGRAMMATICAL
      QUOTE
      EAGLE
      ENTERTAINED
      KISS
      DISENTANGLEMENT
      OCCULTISM

Which of these could be next?

      SCALP
      INCEST
      TAWDRY
      VALETUDINARIANISM

Game 52

The drawings of a motorcyclist repairing his machine are out of order—please correct.

Game 53

1	1	1	1
1	3	5	7
1	5	13	25
1	7	25	

← ?

Can you complete the square logically?

Game 54

These words belong to the same logical family:

> CHINK
> TRANCE
> STAIN
> CHIME
> TUBA
> PERK

Which of these words does too?

> GERMANE
> EMBARGO
> BANANA
> NIGHTMARE

Game 55

Six of the shoes belong to the same logical family. One is an intruder—which one, and why?

GAMES OF LOGIC

Game 56

These words follow a logical progression:

ACE

TAB

COG

ADD

EAR

RAF

GUT

UGH

IVY

TAJ

Which of these could be next?

KID

BOY

ASK

TOO

Game 57

After a long trip abroad, Timothy makes the following statements about the hotels he patronized:

1. When the food is good, the waitresses are gracious.
2. No hotel open all the year long fails to have a view of the ocean.
3. The food is bad only in some cheap hotels.
4. Hotels which have a swimming pool carefully cover their walls with honeysuckle.
5. The hotels where the waitresses are discourteous are those that are open only part of the year.
6. No cheap hotel accepts dogs.
7. Hotels without a swimming pool have no view of the ocean.

In these hotels, can a dog owner enjoy honeysuckle?

Game 58

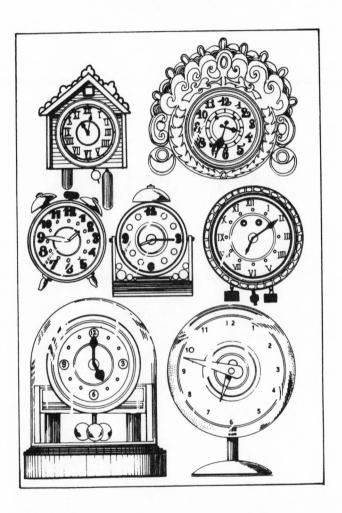

Six of the clocks belong to the same logical family. One is an intruder—which one, and why?

Game 59

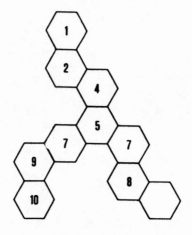

What number belongs in the empty hexagon?

Game 60

Lebrun, Lenoir, and Leblanc are, not necessarily in that order, the accountant, warehouseman, and traveling salesman of a firm.

The salesman, a bachelor, is the shortest of the three.

Lebrun, who is Lenoir's son-in-law, is taller than the warehouseman.

Who has what job?

Game 61

These words follow a logical progression:

ADIEU
IDIOM
EIGHT
UNIPOLAR
PRODUCT
TRUCKLER

Which of these could be next?

PAROCHIALISM
EPISPASTIC
STRICTNESS
OSTEOLOGIC

Game 62

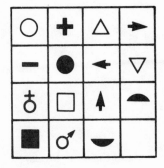

Can you complete the square logically?

Game 63

These words belong to the same logical family:

CALCIFEROUS
CUPELLATION
EDUCATION
LACTIFEROUS
OUTDISTANCE
PNEUMONIA

Which of these words does too?

ZYMOTICALLY
ABSTEMIOUS
UNAPOSTOLIC
MEDALLION

Game 64

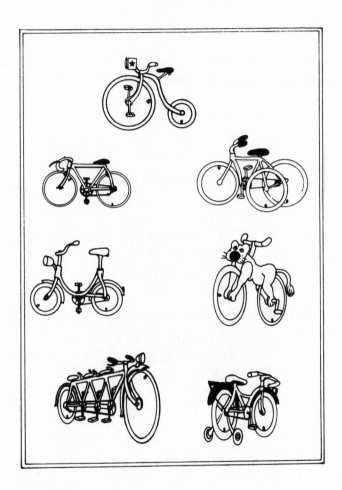

The seven cycles can be put in order, beginning with the starred one on top, according to a logical principle.

What is it? What order should they be in?

Game 65

These words belong to the same logical family:

ADJUNCTIVELY
AMBIDEXTROUS
DEMONSTRABLY
GLANDIFEROUS
HYPNOTIZABLE
QUESTIONABLY

Which of these words does too?

VERSIFICATOR
DIVARICATION
STENOGRAPHIC
EXPOSTULATES

Game 66

Smith is a butcher and president of the street storekeepers' committee, which also includes the grocer, the baker, and the tobacconist. They all sit around a table.

- Smith sits on Smyth's left.
- Smythe sits at the grocer's right.
- Psmith, who faces Smyth, is not the baker.

What kind of store does Smythe have?

Game 67

A driver makes the following statements about automobiles:

- A front-wheel drive gives a good hold on the road.
- It is necessary for a heavy car to have good brakes.
- Any powerful car is high-priced.
- Light cars do not have a good hold on the road.
- A low-powered car cannot have good brakes.

Is it logical for this driver to accept a cheap front-wheel drive?

Game 68

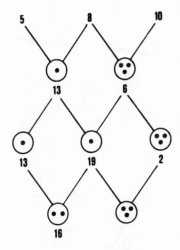

What number belongs under the bottom right circle?

Game 69

Six of these people belong to the same logical grouping. One does not—which one, and why?

GAMES OF LOGIC

Game 70

A history test had three questions on presidents of the United States. Here are the answers of six students:

1. Polk, Polk, Taylor.
2. Taylor, Taylor, Polk.
3. Fillmore, Fillmore, Polk.
4. Taylor, Polk, Fillmore.
5. Fillmore, Taylor, Taylor.
6. Taylor, Fillmore, Fillmore.

Every student answered at least one question correctly. What are the correct answers?

Game 71

After a holdup, four bank employees give descriptions of the robber.

According to the guard, he had blue eyes, was tall, and was wearing a hat and a vest.

According to the cashier, he had dark eyes, was short, and wore a vest and a hat.

According to the secretary, he had green eyes, was medium-sized, and wore a raincoat and a hat.

According to the director, he had gray eyes, was tall, and wore a vest but no hat.

It was later determined that each witness described only one detail out of four correctly. Every detail was described correctly by at least one witness.

What is the correct description of the criminal?

Game 72

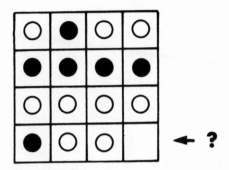

Can you complete the square logically?

Game 73

An explorer is in a country where everyone lives either on the plain or in the mountains. They speak the same language, but the dwellers on the plain always tell the truth while those from the mountains always lie.

The explorer knows little about the language. He knows that "Grb" and "Mnl" mean yes and no but does not know which is which.

He asks three inhabitants of the country two questions each:

- Are both the others from the plain?
- Are both the others from the mountains?

They all answer "Grb" to both questions, except for one who answers "Mnl" to the second question.

What does "Grb" mean?

Game 74

These words belong to the same logical family:

> CODIFY
> LAMINA
> STOVE
> RESET
> JOKUL
> QUIRES

Which of these words does too?

> REST
> GRAIL
> STOIC
> ORDEAL

Game 75

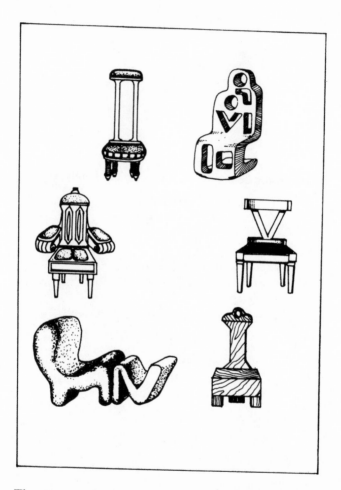

The seats can be put in order according to a logical principle.

What is it? What order should they be in?

Game 76

Timothy has been abandoned by his electrician and must finish the wiring of his new house alone.

He courageously tries to untangle the labyrinth of wires already laid down. He is particularly worried about three wires of the same color going from the basement to the attic. He wants to identify them, labeling both the basement and attic ends of one wire A, of another wire B, and of the last wire C.

His only tool is a meter that shows if current is passing through a length of wire or not when both ends of the wire are attached to the meter. Thanks to it, Timothy only needs to make one round trip between basement and attic to complete the labeling. Explain how he does it.

Game 77

Four couples spend an evening together. Their first names are Elizabeth, Jeanne, Mary, Anne, Henry, Peter, Louis, and Roger.

At a given time:

- Henry's wife is not dancing with her husband, but with Elizabeth's husband.
- Roger and Anne are not dancing.
- Peter is playing the trumpet, with Mary at the piano.

If Anne's husband is not Peter, who is Roger's wife?

Game 78

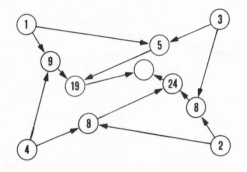

What number belongs in the empty circle?

Game 79

In the small town hall the five members of the council, Anthony, Bernard, Claude, David, and Edwin, are about to elect one of them mayor.

They sit in alphabetical order clockwise around the table.

In the first round everyone votes for the one who votes for his neighbor on the left. Of course, no one is elected. But who voted for whom?

Game 80

These words belong to the same logical family:

TRANSUBSTANTIATION
CRYSTALLOGRAPHICAL
STRAIGHTFORWARDLY
PHILANTHROPICALLY
PARTICULARIZATION
MALADMINISTRATION

Which of these four words does too?

DISPROPORTIONABLE
INCOMMUNICABILITY
MARSIPOBRANCHIATE
DEMONSTRATIVENESS

Game 81

A company whose cash is kept in a strongroom is owned by three associates whose confidence in one another is very limited. They decide to put several locks on the door and to distribute the keys among themselves so that:

- No associate can open the door alone.
- Any two associates can pool their keys to open the door.

How many locks do they need and how many keys?

Game 82

- Some mathematicians are philosophers.
- Immortals are ignorant of philosophy.
- No poet practices mathematics.
- All mortals are poets.

Are these four assertions logically compatible?

Game 83

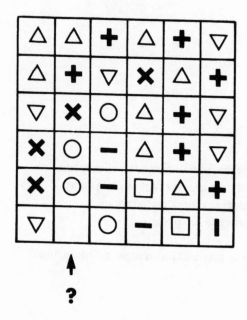

Can you complete the square logically?

GAMES OF LOGIC

Game 84

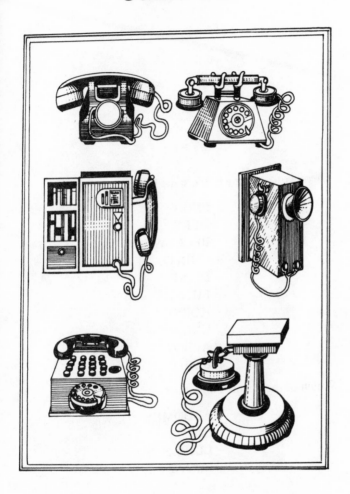

The six telephones can be put in order according to a logical principle.

What is it? What order should they be in?

Game 85

These words belong to the same logical family:

> FIRST
> DEFY
> BELLOW
> CHINTZ
> DEIST
> FILMY
> HORSY
> KNOT
> ABBOT
> BEGIN

Which of these words does too?

> ABDOMEN
> LOW
> EDIBLE
> LOYAL

Game 86

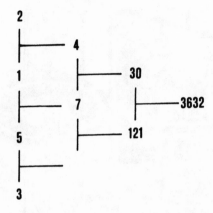

What number belongs in the empty space at the foot of the second column?

Game 87

Six of the portraits belong to the same logical family. One is an intruder—which one, and why?

Game 88

A general is choosing a cook from 625 volunteers. He orders them to form a 25 × 25 square. He orders the tallest man in each row to step aside and chooses the shortest of the twenty-five.

Then he changes his mind and has them go back to their places. He orders the shortest man in each column to step aside and chooses the tallest of *these* twenty-five.

The two cooks chosen by the two methods are different. Which one is taller?

Game 89

These words follow a logical progression:

> JANEY
> FEBRILE

Which of these could be next?

> BEZOAR
> PAVILION
> MAROON
> SEPARATE

Game 90

The staff of a bank includes a director, an assistant director, and four department heads. The director wants to have several locks on the strongroom door and several keys, so that:

- He can open the door alone.
- The assistant director can open it only if he is accompanied by any one of the department heads.
- Any three department heads can open it.

How many locks are needed, and how should the keys be distributed?

Game 91

- Incompetence excludes wisdom.
- Hope can only be founded on knowledge.
- Violence is the last refuge of incompetence.
- To know anything, one must possess wisdom.

What can be deduced about violence from these four assertions?

Game 92

These words belong to the same logical family:

> DIFFICULT
> HUBBUB
> FALLACIOUSLY
> ANTICORROSIVE
> PARAGRAMMATIST
> HOLLOWLY

Which of these words does too?

> SYNTACTICALLY
> INDISCREETNESS
> DEFENDER
> ANNALS

Game 93

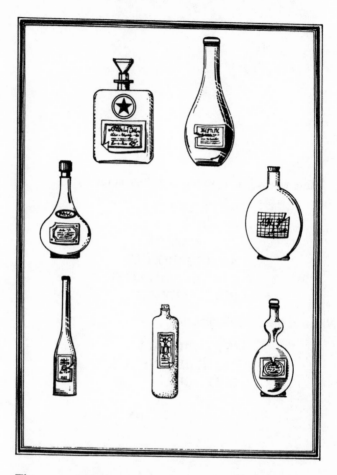

The seven bottles can be put in order, beginning with the starred one and its neighbor to the right, according to a logical principle.

What is it? What order should they be in?

GAMES OF LOGIC

Game 94

Four fishermen, Al, Bert, Claude, and Dick (not neces-sarily respectively), own boats called "Mary Jean," "Susie-Q," "The Big One," and "Seagull."

Unfortunately the fishermen do not know one another as well as they think they do. Each sentence spoken by a fisher-man is true only when it is entirely or partly about his own boat. Otherwise it is false.

Al says: "My boat, 'Susie-Q,' and 'Seagull' are the only ones with radios on board."

Bert says: "Claude is lucky to have one of the three boats with a radio."

Claude says: " 'Seagull' is Al's boat."

Dick says: "I have never been on 'Seagull' or 'Mary Jean.' "

Who owns which boat?

Game 95

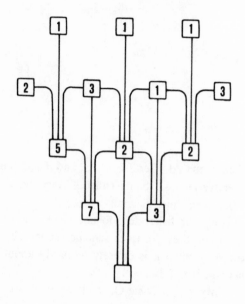

What number belongs in the empty square?

GAMES OF LOGIC

Game 96

Six of the robots belong to the same logical family. One is an intruder—which one, and why?

Game 97

The staff of a bank includes a director, two assistant directors, and five department heads.

The director wants several locks on the strongroom door and several keys so that:

- He can open the door alone.
- An assistant director can only open it together with the other assistant director, *or* with any two department heads.
- Any four department heads can open it.

How many locks are needed and how should the keys be distributed?

Game 98

An explorer is in a country with two villages, a big one and a small one. Although they all speak the same language, the inhabitants of the small village never lie, while those of the big village always lie.

The explorer speaks to a child, pointing to a man and a woman.

"Is the village of this man bigger than the village of this woman?"

"Grb."

"Is your village bigger than the village of this man?"

"Grb."

You don't know whether Grb means yes or no. In fact, you don't need to know. But can you tell what is the correct answer to each question?

Game 99

A plane was returning from the Olympic Games with five athletes who placed first through fifth in an event. They made the following statements:

A: "I was not the last."
B: "C was third."
C: "A was behind E."
D: "E was second."
E: "D was not the first."

On account of modesty or for some other reason, the gold and silver medalists lied. The three worst athletes told the truth.

What order did they all place in?

Game 100

Andrew, Bernard, and Claude are bicycling. Each one is riding the bicycle of one friend and wearing the hat of another.

The one who wears Claude's hat is riding Bernard's bicycle.

Who is riding Andrew's bicycle?

SOLUTIONS

Game 1

30: every arrow adds 2.

Game 2

Take either bar and push one end against the middle of the other bar, forming a T.

If the magnetized bar is the top of the T, there is no pull on the other bar.

Game 3

IODINE: six-letter words with one, two, three, four vowels.

Game 4

Let us call the four drawings:

A   B
C   D

D precedes A and C: the monk's jug has not yet been knocked down.

A precedes C, where the white-booted musketeer is putting his wine-stained hat back on.

B precedes D: the black-booted musketeer has thrown his cloak on the table (he coudn't put it on in the midst of a duel).

The right order is B, D, A, C.

Game 5

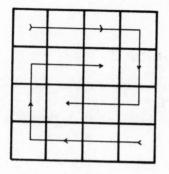

The letters are still in alphabetical order, but simultaneously so, on two symmetrical paths as shown by the arrows.

Game 6

NEEDLESS: two pairs of doubled letters.

Game 7

SUE: The names of each pair contain each of the five vowels once.

Game 8

Each wig has a different number of crossings of strands of hair from one through six.

Game 9

WIGGLE: two A's, B's, C's, D's, E's, F's, G's.

Game 10

A brother is present (without his wife but with his son), and his sister (without her husband but with her daughter).

Game 11

Since the word contains no E or G (as in LEG), the only good letter in ERG is R. Then the good letter of SIR is R, which is the third letter of the desired word. I and L are not in the desired word, so the good letter of AIL is A. The A is not the first letter of the desired word, so it must be the second. The good letter of SIC is C, which must begin the desired word: CAR.

Game 12

512: hexagons with bars yield the square of the preceding number; hexagons with a circle yield half of the preceding number.

Game 13

The intruder (bottom right) is drawn in three strokes of the pen instead of four.

Game 14

There are five colors. The first five ties might be all different colors, but the first six cannot be.

Game 15

HARASS: second, fourth, and sixth letters of each word become first, third, and fifth of the next.

Game 16

Let us call the four drawings:

A   B
C   D

C precedes A, where the tire of the left back wheel of the truck has lost its air.

D precedes B, where the policeman has written more in his notebook.

A precedes D, where the small cloud has been pushed by the wind (the flag shows its direction).

The right order is C, A, D, B.

Game 17

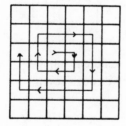

Starting from the center, ABC, ABC, ABC, and so on, has been written along a spiral (arrows).

Game 18

REAPPEARANCE: six vowels and six consonants.

Game 19

Bet on tails. As the coin falls on the table, slap your hand flat on it, saying, "I'd rather see what's underneath so I'll know what didn't come up." You turn the coin over, exposing heads and winning.

But be careful. Your opponent is likely to have two coins, a crooked one for play and a normal one for inspection. If he suspects anything, he may switch them.

Game 20

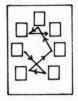

Each door has a different number of vertical lines in its decoration, from one through seven.

Game 21

SATIATE: begin with first three letters of SUNDAY, MONDAY, TUESDAY, WEDNESDAY, THURSDAY, FRIDAY, SATURDAY.

Game 22

The eight letters of EGIS and LOAM are all different; the four letters of the desired word are among them. Then in PLUG, L and G are the good letters, and in ANEW, A and E are the good letters.

The first letters of the four given words include the A, E, and L, so G must be the first letter of the desired word. The third letters of the given words include A and E, so L is the third letter of the desired word. GELA is not a "common English word," so the answer is GALE.

Game 23

The second house from the bottom on the right has ten visible windows instead of nine.

Game 24

11: each number is the sum of the digits in the number or numbers linked to it from above.

Game 25

The top upright car facing left does not have its front wheels turned.

Game 26

The boat. In the water the coin displaces its *volume* of water; in the boat it displaces its *weight* of water. Since coin metal is heavier than water, the coin weighs more than its corresponding volume of water does.

Game 27

DUCAL: vowels alternate with consonants, but successive words begin with a consonant, a vowel, a consonant . . .

Game 28

Let us call the four drawings:

A	B
C	D

The progressive accumulation of hair on the cloth and on the floor leaves only one possible solution:

Timothy wears a wig, and the right order is B, A, D, C.

B: Timothy has just sat down.

A: The hairdresser has taken Timothy's wig off and cut a little of his hair.

D: The haircut is almost over.

C: Timothy has his wig on again and is ready to leave.

Game 29

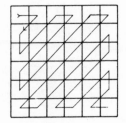

A	A	C	A	E	A
B	B	B	D	B	E
A	C	C	C	D	F
D	B	D	C	G	E
A	E	B	A	D	F
F	A	B	C	G	H

The square is filled, diagonal after diagonal, beginning at the upper left corner (arrows), with the series A, AB, ABC, ABCD, ABCDE, ABCDEF, ABCDEFG, ABCDEFGH.

Game 30

ASHORE: made up of two shorter words, like ACRE, AGE.

Game 31

Yes, it is. Suppose the three friends have run thirty times with these results:
- for the first ten days the order of finish is Timothy, Urban, Vincent.
- for the next ten days it's Urban, Vincent, Timothy.
- for the last ten days it's Vincent, Timothy, Urban.

Timothy finished before Urban twenty days out of thirty. Urban finished before Vincent twenty days out of thirty. Vincent finished before Timothy twenty days out of thirty.

Game 32

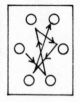

The numbers from 1 through 6 actually appear on each head, disguised as part of the face.

Game 33

ARTERIAL: the two central letters of each word become the first and last letters of the next.

Game 34

Since GUSTO and LIGHT have no good letters, the only good letter in BUILT is B, which begins the desired word. One good letter in BUGLE is B and the other is E (out of place).

The good letters in ADULT are A and D, so the good letter in DYING is D. Y is false, like S, T, and O, so the only good letter in STORY is R, at the correct place. The desired word has the form B . DR . or B . . RD and has to be BEDRA, BEARD, or BAERD. Therefore, it's BEARD.

Game 35

The last fact given means that no one married his son and daughter to the daughter and son of the same friend.

Let us call the five friends by their initials.

"Daughter-in-law of the father of A's son-in-law" means A's daughter. "Son-in-law of the father of C's daughter-in-law" means C's son. Then A's daughter is the sister-in-law of B's son, which can only mean that her brother (A's son) married B's daughter. Similarly, C married his daughter to D's son.

Who is the husband of D's daughter? He cannot be C's or A's son. Let us suppose he is B's son. Then C's daughter's mother-in-law is Mrs. D, while A's son's mother-in-law is Mrs. B. So D's daughter can't have married B's son.

It follows that D's daughter married E's son. D's daughter and B's son have a common mother-in-law: Mrs. E.

Eugene's daughter is married to Bernard's son.

Game 36

24: the number in the center of each circle is the sum of the three numbers on the circumference of the circle.

Game 37

Dickinson is the only one who knows only one of the others. His first name must be Dave.

Bob is neither Dickinson nor Brown. Not knowing Brown, he cannot be Adams nor Carter, so Bob is Emerson.

The first names of the friends at lunch are Alex, Chip, and Elmer. Alex knows Chip and Elmer. Knowing only two friends, he does not know Bob Emerson or Dave Dickinson.

Bob Emerson knows three friends. They are Chip, Dave Dickinson, and Elmer.

Dave Dickinson, knowing only one friend, does not know Chip or Elmer.

Alex and Brown are the only ones to know only two friends. They are the same person: Alex Brown.

Adams's first name is Elmer and Carter's is Chip.

The full names are Elmer Adams, Alex Brown, Chip Carter, Dave Dickinson, and Bob Emerson.

Game 38

The water level remains constant throughout the experiment.

When the ice cube is in the glass, thus floating with the man and the buoy on the water, it displaces its weight of water.

When it falls in the pool it floats again, and still displaces its weight of water.

When it melts it displaces its volume of water. Since it is ice, the volume of water corresponding to its weight is equal to its volume.

Game 39

TENDERNESS: words that sound as if they begin with TWO, FOUR, SIX, EIGHT, TEN.

Game 40

We know that:
- Andrew's house is Belle.
- Bernard's house is Donna.
- Claude's house is Anne.

Their daughters are not so named. Claude cannot be Donna's father and Eugene cannot be Eve's father.

Belle's father, who named his villa Eve, can only be Donald or Eugene.

Similarly, Eve's father is Donald or Eugene. Since he phoned to the last one, he is Donald. His house is Cecilia.

Eugene is Belle's father, Andrew is Donna's father, Bernard is Anne's father, and Claude is Cecilia's father.

Game 41

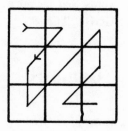

The arrows show how the numbers increase on successive diagonals.

$$1 + 1 = 2$$
$$1 + 2 = 3$$
$$2 + 3 = 5$$
$$3 + 5 = 8$$
$$5 + 8 = 13$$
$$8 + 13 = 21$$

The number in each square is the sum of the numbers in the two preceding squares—a Fibonacci series. The last square contains $13 + 21 = 34$.

Game 42

HIJACKER: three consecutive letters in alphabetical order.

Game 43

Each group of twenty-one persons speaking a language has four subgroups: (1) three languages, (2) two languages, (3) another two-language subgroup (for example, English and German as opposed to French and German in the German group), and (4) one language. There are only three ways of equating twenty-one with four numbers that are all different and all greater than 2:

$$21 = 3 + 4 + 6 + 8$$
$$= 3 + 5 + 6 + 7$$
$$= 3 + 4 + 5 + 9$$

The last line contains the largest of the subgroups, who speak only French (9); so the last line is the French-speaking group.

The number of those who speak English and German but not French must appear as a subgroup on both of the first two lines, that is, as 3 or 6. But this is also true of the subgroup speaking all three languages; this latter must be 3, since 6 does not appear on the last line. So there are six conferees who speak English and German but not French.

Game 44

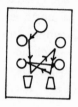

Each vase has a different number of crossings of lines at right angles, rising by twos from two through fourteen.

Game 45

GENEROUS: two vowels and S, preceded by zero, one, two, three, four, five, letters.

Game 46

We can reorder and restate the statements as follows:
1. If a strategist is a good tactician, he is never vanquished.
2. If a strategist is audacious, he has the confidence of his troops.
3. If a strategist has the confidence of his troops, he is a good tactician. (If he were bad, he would not have their confidence.)
4. If a strategist is never vanquished, he is not despised by women.

Therefore, if a strategist is audacious, he is not despised by women.

Game 47

From Mrs. D's second assertion we know that A is the stepfather of X (who remains to be identified), who is the stepfather of B.

From her first assertion: D is the stepfather of Y, who is the stepfather of Z, who is the stepfather of E.

From her third assertion: C is the stepfather of R, who is the stepfather of S, who is the stepfather of T, who is the stepfather of F.

We know that Mrs. D is not C's mother, for she is speaking to her. There is only one solution that fits these facts: A is the stepfather of D, who is the stepfather of B, who is the stepfather of F, who is the stepfather of E, who is the stepfather of C, who is the stepfather of A.

Game 48

8: each knot yields (below it) the sum of the two horizontal numbers minus the number above the knot.

Game 49

We know that Deer missed a roe and killed a hare. Since Roe did not miss a roe (same name), he did not kill a deer. Likewise, the deer cannot have been killed by Deer or missed by Roe.

Since Hare did not miss a hare or a roe, the doe was not killed by Hare or by Roe, or by Doe. Hence the doe was not missed by Hare.

Only Boar can have killed a doe. Then Hare missed a boar and Roe missed a doe. The deer was killed by Doe and the roe by Hare.

Game 50

The younger son plays one game every two days.

Game 51

INCEST: number of letters in each word is the number in the alphabet of the first letter of the next word. The first word has twenty-six letters, so the second word begins with Z, the twenty-sixth letter in the alphabet, and so on.

Game 52

Let us call the four drawings:

A   B
C   D

C precedes B, which shows a new stain on the right leg.

D precedes A, which shows a new stain on the chin and cheek.

A precedes C, which shows a new stain on the chest.

The right order is D, A, C, B.

(The state of the motorcycle parts is inconclusive, for a motorcycle can be taken apart as well as put together.)

Game 53

Each number is the sum of three numbers:
- above.
- above left.
- left.

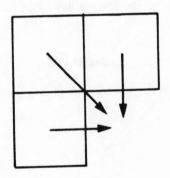

The missing number is 63.

Game 54

GERMANE: change one letter in each word to get a country (CHINA, FRANCE, SPAIN, CHILE, CUBA, PERU, GERMANY).

Game 55

Three shoes have low heels and laces, and three have high heels and no laces. The seventh has a high heel and laces.

Game 56

KID: begin with A, end with B, begin with C, end with D...

Game 57

We can reorder and restate Timothy's opinions as follows:

6. If the hotel accepts dogs, its prices are high.
3. If prices are high, the food is good.
1. If the food is good, the waitresses are courteous.
5. If the waitresses are courteous, the hotel is open all year long.
2. If a hotel is open all year long, it has a view of the ocean.
7. If there is a view of the ocean, there is a swimming pool.
4. If there is a swimming pool, there is honeysuckle on the walls.

Therefore, hotels that accept dogs have honeysuckle on the walls.

Game 58

Six clocks have their hands in correct positions, but the hour hand of the seventh clock shows about "ten of" while the minute hand shows "ten after."

Game 59

10: numbers increase by 1 if they go down vertically and by 2 if they go down diagonally.

Game 60

Lebrun is taller than the warehouseman, so he is not the warehouseman or the salesman. He is the accountant.

The salesman is not Lebrun and not Lenoir (a married man). He is Leblanc.

By elimination, Lenoir is the warehouseman.

Game 61

PAROCHIALISM: one, two, three, four, five, six, seven consonants.

Game 62

Imagine the square is cut onto four squares. Their diagonals have opposite symbols:

- plus—minus;
- black circle—white circle;
- black square—white square, etc.

The missing symbol is a downward-pointing arrow.

Game 63

ABSTEMIOUS: each of the five vowels appears once.

Game 64

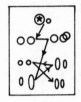

Each cycle has the front wheel's tire valve in a different position, rotating forward by about an eighth of a turn per drawing.

Game 65

STENOGRAPHIC: no letter appears twice.

Game 66

Assigning Smith the bottom seat, the four men can only sit this way:

SMYTHE

PSMITH   SMYTH

SMITH

Hence Smyth is the grocer, Psmith is the tobacconist, and Smythe is the baker.

Game 67

No. He says that if there is a front-wheel drive, the car has a good hold on the road; if so, it is heavy; if so, it has good brakes; if so, it is powerful; and if so, it is high-priced.

Game 68

7: The number under each circle is the sum of the number or numbers above that are linked to the circle, divided by the number of dots inside the circle.

Game 69

The man at top left wears eight visible pieces of cloth instead of seven.

Game 70

Note that the three correct answers need not all be different.

Can the first answer be Polk? If so, only #1 answered the question correctly. Then #3 and #4 must each be right on one of the last two questions, where the answers must be either Fillmore or Polk. But #5 must be right on one of these questions too, although he answered Taylor to both. This is impossible, so the first answer is not Polk.

Can the first answer be Fillmore? If so, by similar reasoning on the answers of #1 and #2, the last two answers must be either Polk or Taylor; but #6 answered Fillmore to both. Still another impossibility.

By elimination, the correct first answer is Taylor. Then the second answer is Fillmore and the third is Taylor again.

Game 71

Let us tabulate the descriptions:

	Eyes	Size	Coat	Hat
Guard	blue	tall	vest	yes
Cashier	dark	short	vest	yes
Secretary	green	medium	raincoat	yes
Director	gray	tall	vest	no

Not more than one witness can be right about any detail, or there would have to be another detail that no witness is right about. Therefore, the criminal did not wear a hat. The director was right about that and thus wrong about everything else, so the criminal had no vest, was not tall and did not have gray eyes. The only detail the guard can have right is the blue eyes. The correct detail of the cashier is that the robber was short; that of the secretary is that he wore a raincoat.

The criminal was blue-eyed and short, wearing a raincoat and bareheaded.

Game 72

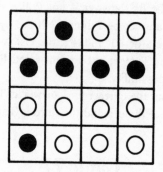

In each successive 2 × 2 square, top left, top right, bottom left, bottom right, there is one more white circle.

Game 73

The three inhabitants can't be all from the plain or all from the mountains, or all the answers would be the same.

Can there be two from the mountains and one from the plain? No, for they would all answer yes to the second question.

Therefore there are two from the plain and one from the mountains. They all say no to the first question. At the second question, those from the plain say no and the one from the mountains says yes.

Then "Grb" means no.

Game 74

REST: contains three consonants, which are consecutive consonants in the alphabet.

Game 75

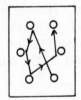

Looked at closely, every seat shows a roman number, from I through VI.

Game 76

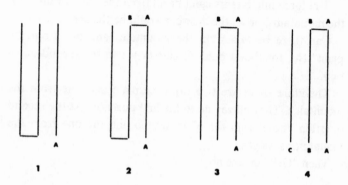

In the basement Timothy fastens any two of the three wires together. He labels the free wire A.

In the attic, Timothy tests every pair of wires with the meter—that is, three possible pairings. The pair the current goes through is the one fastened in the basement. The leftover wire is A's other end and must be labeled A too. Timothy then fastens A to a randomly chosen wire of the pair, which he labels B. The third wire is labeled C.

Back in the basement, Timothy unfastens the two wires and tests all three possible parts of wires with the meter. The pair with current is fastened in the attic, and the wire not labeled A must be labeled B. The third is labeled C.

Game 77

Elizabeth's husband is not Henry. He cannot be Roger or Peter, who are not dancing, so Elizabeth is married to Louis.

Likewise, Henry's wife is not Elizabeth, or Anne, or Mary. Henry is married to Jeanne.

Peter's wife is Mary.

Roger's wife is Anne.

Game 78

62: each circle (except the corner ones) is the target of two arrows, one long and one short. The number in each circle is the number the short arrow comes from plus twice the number the long arrow comes from.

Game 79

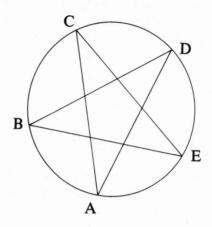

Since no one is elected, "his" refers to the same person as "everyone" in the last paragraph.

Let us consider Anthony's case. He can't vote for himself: he would vote for his left neighbor too.

Anthony can't vote for Bernard, because Bernard is Anthony's left neighbor and that would mean Anthony has to vote for himself too, which is contradictory.

Anthony can't vote for Claude: Claude would have to vote for Anthony's left neighbor Bernard, Bernard for David, David for Claude, and Claude for Edwin, which is contradictory.

Anthony can't vote for Edwin. Edwin would vote for Bernard, Bernard for Anthony, and Anthony for Claude, which is contradictory.

Anthony can only vote for David, who votes for Bernard, who votes for Edwin, who votes for Claude, who votes for Anthony.

Game 80

INCOMMUNICABILITY: none of these long words contains an E.

Game 81

Three locks and three keys are enough. Let the keys be A, B, and C. The first associate gets keys A and B; the second associate keys B and C; and the third associate keys C and A.

Now each associate has only two keys out of three. He cannot open the door alone, but can with the help of either other associate.

Game 82

From the second statement, philosophers are mortals (or they would be ignorant of philosophy).

Since all mortals are poets, philosophers are poets.

Since no poet practices mathematics, no philosopher does either.

Then a mathematician cannot be a philosopher. The four assertions are inconsistent.

Game 83

△   △ ✚   △ ✚ ▽   △ ✚ ▽ ✘   •••

Reading horizontally from left to right, line by line, there is a series of one symbol, then two, three, and so on. Once the nth symbol in a series is established it does not change. The missing symbol, being fourth in such a series, is **X**.

Game 84

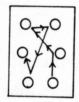

Each phone cord makes a different number of loops, from one through six.

Game 85

LOW: letters of each word are in alphabetical order.

Game 86

17: to the right of each horizontal T is the product of the two numbers at the left plus 2.

Game 87

Three portraits have a beard in a rectangular frame, and three have no beard in an oval frame. The portrait at bottom right has no beard in a rectangular frame.

Game 88

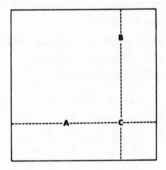

Let A be the first cook and B the second.

If A and B are in the same row, A is taller.

Likewise, if A and B are in the same column, B is shorter.

If they are in different columns and rows, let C be the volunteer in A's row and B's column. C is shorter than A, but taller than B.

So A is always taller than B.

Game 89

MAROON: begin with first three letters of JANUARY, FEBRUARY, MARCH.

Game 90

It is simpler to consider which keys are *not* given to whom.

The director gets the keys to all the locks and need not be considered further.

Let A, B, C, D, and E be the assistant director and the four department heads.

A gets all the keys but one, and B, C, D, and E all get the key A doesn't get. Now only the remaining keys of B, C, D, and E need be considered.

Each group of two department heads should lack one key. There are six such groups, so seven keys are needed.

Here is the distribution of keys:

X	A	B	C	D	E
1		1	1	1	1
2	2			2	2
3	3		3		3
4	4		4	4	
5	5	5			5
6	6	6		6	
7	7	7	7		

Game 91

Violence is accompanied by incompetence, which excludes wisdom, without which there is no knowledge and, therefore, no hope.

Game 92

ANNALS: doubled consonant between identical vowels.

Game 93

On each label a small part is folded or torn. Its position turns clockwise from bottle to bottle.

Game 94

Al mentions his own boat, so it is true that "Susie-Q" and "Seagull" have radios. Also they don't belong to him.

"Seagull" can't belong to Claude, or his sentence would be true, and he couldn't say the boat belongs to Al.

Likewise, Dick can't own "Seagull" or "Mary Jean." Bert owns "Seagull."

"Seagull" has a radio. Then Bert's sentence is true, for, like Al, he mentions three boats with a radio; so Claude does have a radio. Since Claude can't own Al's boat or "Seagull," he owns "Susie-Q."

"The Big One" belongs to Dick and "Mary Jean" to Al.

Game 95

19: the number in each square is the product of the numbers in the northeast and northwest squares minus the number in the north square.

Game 96

A robot's head, hands, and feet can each be shaped like a human being's or not. Six robots have two human elements (head, hands; or head, feet; or hands, feet). The middle robot at the right has only a human-shaped head.

Game 97

Twenty locks are needed. The director owns all the keys. Each assistant director should lack five keys, one in common with each department head. (The two sets of five keys should not overlap.) Each group of three department heads should lack one key. There are ten such groups, so $10 + 5 + 5 = 20$ keys are distributed.

Here are the keys that are *not* given to assistant directors A and B and to department heads C, D, E, F, and G:

A	B	C	D	E	F	G
1		1				
2			2			
3				3		
4					4	
5						5
	6	6				
	7		7			
	8			8		
	9				9	
	10					10
		11	11	11		
		12		12	12	
		13			13	13
		14	14	14		
		15	15			15
		16		16		16
			17	17	17	
			18		18	18
			19	19		19
				20	20	20

Game 98

The matrix shows what the child will answer (truthfully on lines 2, 4, 6, 8; falsely on lines 1, 3, 5, 7), for all eight residence possibilities:

Village of man	Village of woman	Village of child	First answer	Second answer
big	big	big	yes	yes
big	big	small	no	no
big	small	big	no	yes
big	small	small	yes	no
small	big	big	yes	no
small	big	small	no	no
small	small	big	yes	no
small	small	small	no	no

Only lines 1, 2, 6, and 8, where the first and second answers are identical, can actually occur. In each of these four cases, the village of the man is not bigger than the village of the woman. So the correct first answer is no.

In the same four cases, the village of the child is not bigger than the village of the man. So the correct second answer is also no. (This does not mean, however, that the child said no. In the case of line 1, he said yes; in the other three cases he said no.)

Game 99

A's statement must be true: if he is lying, he is last and he is also first or second, which is contradictory. So A is third or fourth.

If D is telling the truth, E is lying and D is first and is lying, which is contradictory. So E is not second, and D is first or second.

If E is lying, D is first and E second. But D is lying when he says E is second. Therefore, E is telling the truth, which makes him third, fourth, or fifth. D is not first, but second.

Only B or C can be first. If B is not first, since he is also not second he is telling the truth, and C is third, and cannot be first either, which is impossible. Then B is first and C is not third.

C, being neither first nor second, is telling the truth that A is behind E. E is third, A is fourth, and C is fifth.

The athletes placed in this order: B, D, E, A, C.

Game 100

The person riding Bernard's bicycle and wearing Claude's hat can't be Bernard or Claude: he is Andrew.

If Bernard is riding Andrew's bicycle, Claude is riding his own. He is not, so Bernard is riding Claude's bicycle and Claude is riding Andrew's.

About the Author

Born in Tours, France, Pierre Berloquin was trained as an operations research engineer, which gave him an excellent background in mathematics and logical thinking. His popular column on "Games and Paradoxes" appears twice monthly in *The World of Science*, a supplement of the Paris newspaper, *Le Monde*.